HOW TO TALK DIRTY:

THE BEGINNER'S GUIDE TO TALK DIRTY WITH YOUR PARTNER.

CHANGE YOUR WORDS, CHANGE YOUR SEX.

Joanne Bennet

Table of contents

not engaging in the rendering of legal, financial, medical or professional advice. The content within this book has been derived from various sources. Please consult a licensed professional before attempting any techniques outlined in this book.

By reading this document, the reader agrees that under no circumstances is the author responsible for any losses, direct or indirect, which are incurred as a result of the use of information contained within this document, including, but not limited to, — errors, omissions, or inaccuracies.

Introduction

First, understand that a sexual relationship between two consenting adults has its ups and downs. For example, marriage is meant to be the happy union of two adults who love and support each other. However, many marriages are either not as the individuals expected them to be or are on the verge of a divorce. One of the major reasons for the unhappiness and misunderstandings in marriages is the communication gap between couples. And nothing widens the communication gap in marriages more than a lack of physical and emotional intimacy. And often those intimacies are connected as the quality of emotional intimacy can quickly deteriorate if physical intimacy is always a boring routine.

The closer couples get physically, the easier they can communicate their concerns, fears, worries, doubts, and hopes to each other. Sex is one of the natural ways physical intimacy can be greatly improved between couples. If you have sex great, exciting, and a fun activity you and your partner look forward to you both automatically improving your physical and emotional closeness. You also improve the quality of your communication. If you can freely tell your partner how you want to be pleasured and what you want to do to them sexually, it will be a lot easier to share with them whatever other concerns you have in life and in the relationship.

1

Now that you get the general idea of it, let us go into a bit more detail about all the reasons you should consider including dirty talk into your sexual relationship.

1. It allows you to communicate what you want: Saying what you want during sex is vital for your enjoyment. Telling your partner how much you enjoy what they are doing when they are doing it will encourage them to do it more. "I love it when you do that," tells your partner to keep doing whatever it is they are doing. Sitting down to have a conversation about what your sexual preferences are can take away the fun and spontaneity from sex. But dirty talk can communicate the same preferences without making as big of an issue out of it as it would be in a normal conversation.

2. It helps your partner to know what is on your mind: Not many people can read minds. Your partner may be giving their all but doing all the wrong things and still thinking they are giving you pleasure. If you do not speak up, they probably will not know. Sex, for many people, is a riddle that they cannot solve. What does he mean by that facial expression? Is that moaning a good sign or a bad one? Does she want me to continue doing that or what? Instead of enjoying the act, many people spend time guessing what the other person wants because they are not saying what is on their mind. You can start with things like, "Come up a bit. No, to the left. Apply a bit more pressure." These may not be dirty talks, but it is a start. If you can break the silence and tell each

other what you will prefer and exactly how you want it, saying how good it makes you feel can easily follow. For example, "No, to the left. That is the spot! It feels so good when you stroke it like that."

3. It strengthens your connection: Vocalizing your sexual fantasies and desires requires a lot of trust in the other person. Sharing something that can be potentially embarrassing is letting your partner know that you are not afraid to be vulnerable with them. It shows them that you trust them enough to share your intimate thoughts with them. Doing this can make your connection to your partner stronger.

4. It is great foreplay: Foreplay is essential for arousal, especially in women. It takes a comparatively long time for women to get sexually turned on than it does for men. As a result, the more varied you can make foreplay, the sexier a woman feels, and the wilder the sex. Dirty talk is another level of foreplay that can turn women (and men) on even before making any physical contact.

5. It is foreplay for anywhere and anytime: You can talk dirty all day even when you are miles apart. Texts, phone calls, and photos can be used to keep the mind stimulated and ready for physical sex throughout the day. A short text such as "Can't wait to get a feel of your sexy body," can keep your partner in the mood throughout the day.

6. It reignites your passion: If you have been in a relationship with someone for a while, it is unrealistic to think that the level of lust you once had for them will continue to remain unwaveringly strong throughout your relationship. Love and lust in a sexual relationship can last forever but not without some work. Those feelings can decline with time, but you can reignite them with dirty talk. So, if it feels like your sex life has become one dreary, predictable script, spice it up with some dirty talks.

7. It keeps your juices flowing: Yes, both your sexual juices and creative juices flow better with dirty talk. Instead of being stuck in your sexual imaginations, you can vocalize the pictures in your head. The more you describe what you want to do, the better your creativity gets. Who knows, you may even act out those fantasies.

8. It improves your self-confidence: Attempting something as challenging as dirty talk can help to boost your self-confidence. And your confidence will not just be limited to the bedroom, but it will also rub off on other aspects of your life. Try to remember the first time you fell deeply in love with someone new. Your whole body felt lighter, there was an invisible spring that carried you effortlessly when you walked, and you approached almost all your tasks as if they were all easy. You were not afraid to face anything because of how you felt inwardly. That is the power of self-confidence. And you can get a good dose of it by overcoming your shyness in the bedroom.

9. Lessens performance pressure: Leaving your partner clueless during sex can lead to the annoying and self-conscious question, "Am I doing it right?" Your partner may retort in their head, "Just shut up and get this over with!" There is nothing wrong if your partner checks in to know if you are comfortable with something they are doing. But when it becomes too frequent, it is usually an indication of performance pressure. It shows that your partner does not know whether they are doing what you want or not. It also shows that they are trying to please you instead of enjoying themselves while pleasuring you. But when both of you learn to vocalize your desires and are willing to understand each other's sexual preferences, it takes away the pressure of performance and makes you both relax into the moment.

10. It creates better sex and new experiences: Of course, with all the benefits listed above, it is only logical that talking dirty leads to better sex. Since there are hardly any secrets between the couple (at least regarding sex), it is easier to let go and enjoy better sex. But besides the great intercourse, it can also lead to trying out new things such as toys, new sex positions, role-playing, and fun things you never imagined you were capable of. Of course, not everyone wants to switch into kinky sex, but regardless of how modest you are, talking dirty gives you more room to vary your sexual experiences to make them wilder and more mind-blowing.

Silent sex is boring! There is hardly any sexual activity without words and images popping into the mind. Vocalizing what goes on in the mind creates more excitement than keeping mute. Without words, it is like being physically present with your partner but mentally absent.

Why both men and women like dirty talk has a lot to do with how the human brain functions. Everyone who engages in sex likes to be pleasured in a way that deeply satisfies their bodily needs. Being able to say exactly how that need should be satisfied and hearing how your partner wants theirs to be met can turn both of you on.

How to Introduce It to Your Partner?

Some people, mostly women, become so self-conscious that they find it difficult to remain mentally present during sex. They are worried about their nakedness or the shape of their body parts. Talking dirty keeps their attention rooted in the moment. When the man says, "I love kissing your hard nipples," for example, it automatically draws the woman's attention to her nipples and makes her feel the sensation in that part of her body.

On the other hand, a man is generally turned on by a confident woman. A woman who can boldly say what she is going to do to him, or who wants to know how he prefers to be treated sexually, is confident. When a woman begs during sex, it boosts the man's ego and can make him last longer, perform more passionately, and do what she wants and desires.

Curse words and profanity may be viewed as offensive and an uncultured way of communication. But inside the bedroom and in the context of sexual relations, it could be a turn on depending on what the individuals prefer.

The idea that dirty talk is for perverts is incorrect. There is nothing wrong with wanting a heightened sexual experience or vocalizing what is on your mind. Men love to hear women please and tease them verbally, and women love to hear men appreciate their bodies and sexuality. These are all perfectly healthy things to desire and practice. Talking dirty is all about sex – and there is nothing wrong with sex between two consenting adults. In any case, sex is supposed to be erotic, dirty, and even filthy, but most importantly, sex is meant to be fun. There is no reason that sex talks should be limited to only "appropriate" and "morally correct" words or phrases.

Talking dirty is about filling in the blanks by two people engaged in sex or foreplay. For example, one person says, "I like it when you (....)" and the other person says, "I love your (....)" When two people do the dirty talking, it gets crazier with each exchange and their sex experience intensifies accordingly.

The bottom line is this: If the only sounds you can hear during sex are the creak of the bed, the sound of your bodies rubbing against each other, and deep breaths, you are leaving out a vital piece of the fun. You should be hearing words of appreciation, commands, pleas, and so on, coupled with those moans and sighs of deep satisfaction.

A lot of people want to introduce more fun and excitement in their sexual relationships, and that is okay. However, if done incorrectly, it can backfire. It is not enough to want things to change in the bedroom. How you introduce the change can be the difference between acceptance and rejection.

Now that we have seen the benefits of dirty talk and how our psychological makeup supports it, let us consider how to safely introduce it to your partner. This process is particularly vital for several reasons. It could be that:

- Neither of you has tried talking dirty before.

- Your partner is the sexually reserved type.

- Everyday pressure has eroded the sexual passion you both shared when you were younger lovers.

Whatever the case, learning to safely introduce or reintroduce dirty talks into your relationship is not rocket science. However, since personal values or boundaries are involved, emotions and feelings can get out of hand, and moods can suddenly be ruined, it is crucial to approach it carefully.

How to Talk Dirty with Your Partner?

Why Dirty Talk?

You may be perusing this because your partner has communicated an enthusiasm for hearing devious words. And you may in return, hungers for those affectionate words. Possibly you need to liven up your sex life, or perhaps you are only inquisitive concerning why your accomplice likes to talk such a great amount in bed. Perhaps you are effectively an incredible dirty talker who needs another thought or two, or perhaps you are simply in the disposition to look over on your underhanded skills. Whatever the explanation, you have picked the correct course to get what you need!

Talking dirty has become such a lot of some portion of our sexual culture that it has produced studies, interviews, gatherings, and research aplenty. Truth be told before it was designated "dirty talk," the specialty of directing sexual sentiments toward your lover with the plan to stir had a logical name: Lagnolalia.

There is a valid justification for this logical intrigue. Over 80% of our sex life happens in our minds, which means that dream, memory, and want are the absolute most impressive driving powers behind all that we do behind shut entryways. Studies have demonstrated that when you get physical with your partner, your mind has been paving the way to the experience.

So why not go for the dirty talk? It is been in the rear of your brain the entire day anyway! As per Aline P. Zoldbrod, Ph.D., the writer of wickedness, sexy talk with your accomplice not just fires up play between the sheets yet enhances your life in ways you would never have envisioned.

It causes your accomplice to feel great to realize how energized you are, and your excitement causes them to feel like the best lover on the planet. That may clarify why dirty talk makes you shiver in all the privilege places; however, it does not clarify why the naughtiest dirty talk can likewise be the most smoking. It is one comment "fuck" what is more, get a grin, yet it's very another to tell your accomplice precisely how you need to screw them in the most realistic terms you can envision.

The dirtier the words, the better. What is up with that?
Single-word: Taboo.

From the time we are small kids, we are instructed not to state dirty words. Expressing devious things is not what great young ladies or young men do. Breaking that unthinkable with an accomplice causes you to feel like you are defying the norms, and that this way causes you to feel braver.

At the point when the room entryway closes behind you and those dirty words come out of your mouth, the cultural shows vanish. You may become flushed like distraught, and you may even get somewhat neurotic and marvel what would occur on the off chance that anybody, God restrict, heard you talking this way! You might even get bothered and not have the option to talk over a murmur. That is when you know you have quite recently separated an obstruction you probably will not have known was there in any case.

The best dirty talk kicks open an even more extensive entryway with one significant question: If you can speak profanely in bed, what else would you be able to do? Talking dirty opens entryways, you never at any point knew were there!

Express talk is a certainty promoter, as well. In addition to the fact that it makes him hot to find out about the things you need to do with him, it likewise gives you the satisfaction of knowing how completely you have turned your accomplice on. The naughtier you talk, the sexier you feel. That sexiness does not leave when you leave the room, and the certainty you pull from that overflows into everything else you do.

Above all, talking dirty allows you to voice what you truly need in bed, regardless of whether it be with blooming language or obtuse and to the point – in any case, it increments your possibility of sexual fulfillment.

Closeness is the passionate association, what is more, the reaction you have to your accomplice. The most sizzling tumble is nothing contrasted with the sizzling warmth that comes when closeness is included. Being alright with your accomplice, anxious to kindly and prepared to open a piece of yourself to him is the way to incredible sex life.

In any case, that is only the beginning of the great stuff. As closeness manufacturers, our restraints drop. The more agreeable you become with your sexuality, the more likely you are to grasp each perspective of it, even those you may have once thought about forbidden. Amidst profound closeness, what was once terrifying can be enabling.

Talking dirty resembles imparting a mystery to your accomplice, one that you two know and comprehend. At the point when you are out on the town in broad daylight, introducing your best face to the world, no one yet your accomplice realizes how shrewd you can truly be.

At the point when you face your colleagues or your chief or specialist or any other person, besides, they have no clue about the genuine individual you become at the point when you are sleeping with your lover. Your accomplice is the one who sees all the concealed sides of you. What a thrill, knowing there is something so extraordinary that solitary you two offer, furthermore, nobody else would ever figure! As you figure out how to speak profanely, it opens a different universe of probability. You will most likely learn things about your accomplice that you never envisioned, and it is a certain wager he will adapt very somewhat about you!

Basic Guidelines of Talking Dirty

1. Slow and steady wins the race

Unfortunately, this is where most persons get it wrong. The beginning of everything matters a lot. Even in the main sexual act, both partners cannot just remove their clothes and go straight to grinding each other. What we should understand is that for the body to react and respond to the very way we want it to be, it must be warmed up somehow until it gradually gets heated to the kind of level we want.

2. The bedroom is the perfect place, but not the only place

For beginners, it is advisable that you start your erotic talk in the bedroom; that is only if the situation allows it. The reason being that beginners are always too concerned about their privacy. So, to avoid you feeling that much tension, and at the same time so you will be able to completely relax and not think about anything else other than your partner, the bedroom is most likely the best place.

3. Hide behind the screen and say your mind

In most situations this can precede other talking dirty guidelines depending on the nature of things between the partners involved. Now, this too can be of utmost help not only to beginners but every person out there. Well, if you are really terrified about talking dirty and you do not really see yourself doing it anytime soon; then the best way to go about it is through a text.

4. Practice makes perfect

This might sound hilarious but trust me if you are not that comfortable, practicing in front of a mirror is not out of place. I know this sounds very silly and you probably think you will look stupid while you are doing it, practice in front of the mirror before facing the crowd. Just like them, you would not want to disappoint.

5. See what they like

How do you expect someone to go literally crazy for you when all you spit out or do is what they dislike or does not even mean anything to them? Let us face it, there is no one who doesn't like going a bit naughty every now and then, but the catch is that we all love different things. You cannot expect what works for 'A' to also trigger 'B'.

6. Be intentional and most importantly be a part of the process

There is virtually no essence trying to talk dirty if you do not like it. The main reason for talking dirty is so that both partners enjoy it. If one finds it irritating, then the whole essence is defeated. There are people that have problems using explicit languages, so in such situations, trying to talk dirty might not end well. Try it first and then decide if both of you like it or not.

7. Have limit

Nowadays, due to technological advancement and emergence of social media, talking dirty is almost like nothing. Even a teenager can spit out vulgar words all in the name of talking dirty. We barely have innocent and mild erotic talk. It is worthy to note that if there's lack of trust, then you should not be involving yourself in talking dirty with such a person. You would not want something you said over in chats or call to be used against you.

8. Creativity is the key

Research is very vital in our daily living. Reading and searching for helpful videos about things you want to improve upon is a big step in providing solutions to problems. In one word, all I am trying to say is be original.

9. Know when to stop

The truth is that if things are not going in the direction you want them to, try something else. You should know when to stop. Talking dirty should not be out of compulsion. You do not have to insist on erotic talk if your partner is just not in the mood for it. There is also a chance that you might say something irritating in the process. Humanly, things get irritating when someone is not in the right frame of mind. Hence, it is better to leave it than force it because if you force it the outcome might not be pleasurable at all.

10. Try to be in control

When I say be the dominant one, I am not only referring to the males alone. Usually men like to take this role, but also majority of them love their women being in charge. As a lady, if you need a mind-blowing sex then you should try to take the lead soon enough. You will be surprised to know how much men fall for this sweet trap. Do not fear what to say; dirty talk appears naturally once you are ready to take charge.

11. Be descriptive. Tell him/her what you want

What I really do not understand is what could possibly cause two partners to be shy of each other. Honestly, I do not see any big deal in telling your significant other how you want to be fucked. Yes, there is nothing serious in that. Instead of the normal "I want you to have sex with me", you could give details to make it sound better and more arousing. By sounding better, the results are going to be better, too.

12. Don't just say anything that comes to mind, choose your words carefully

Talking dirty is as simple as a piece of cake; it is not that difficult. It is all about speaking your mind and telling your partner things you want them to do to you, without any shame and with huge sexual tension. The best way to do this is to feel how they breathe in a non-sexual environment. Choose those moments to ask him if there are any words, they do not want you to use.

Therefore, never limit yourself to using this language only in the bedroom. Like I said earlier, there's life outside the bedroom. There is a first time for everything, so try to allow talking dirty with your significant other to be a common part of your daily life.

What Women Wants?

It is clear that each person is a world and each one makes us enjoy different things in bed. It is also known to all the fact that women enjoy orgasms to a much lesser extent than men and this results in many who end up pretending to encourage - or not discourage - their partners or even shy away from sex because they enjoy the just thing.

But there is a whole world of possibilities for women to have a great time during a sex session. And, to get it, you probably have to start thinking Ask Men, "in sex, women come first."

Do not fool yourself, it is not possible to establish a specific method for women to reach orgasm nor is there a magic button that makes them enjoy immediately. But some advice can be given about attitudes and movements that help them, in general, enjoy more during sexual intercourse.

You can have really satisfying relationships; you just have to try to fulfil some of the hidden desires of the women.

IT ACTS AS A 'COMMAND', NOT AS A 'SWITCH'

Male and female sexuality are entirely different: while men are like light switches - just by lying on them are they ready to go to work - women need to be activated little by little. Hence the always underlined importance of the preliminaries, women are like baking a soufflé: the result depends on the ingredients and if the chef is sure of what he does, but also the reliability of the oven, temperature, humidity.

GET A STATE OF CALM AND COMFORT

The key to a woman activating in bed and reaching orgasm is to feel a deep sense of relaxation, the parts of the female brain responsible for processing fear, anxiety and emotions were deactivated when they were more excited producing a trance state during the climax. "The deactivation makes the sensations that could be the key to reach orgasm disappear. In the case of men, on the contrary, hardly any alteration was perceived in these regions.

SEE LITTLE BY LITTLE WHAT WORKS

Every woman is different, and most do not even reach orgasm during their first sexual encounters with a man. The objective is that they feel comfortable and to do this, finding out what excites and stimulates them can be the key: and be careful because not everyone likes the same thing.

TRY NEW THINGS: TAKE YOUR IMAGINATION

As we said, it is good to know the path that never fails, but they also expect it to be innovated in bed. Once you have enough confidence in bed surprises become essential. It is precisely the people who enjoy a satisfying sex life who have more hidden desires.

EXPLOIT YOUR STRENGTHS

Very few people make love like porn stars. We live in the real world and we all have sexual strengths and weaknesses, we must learn to alleviate our deficiencies: For example, I suffered premature ejaculation for years and compensated for it through oral sex.

BECOME A CLITORIAN

To embark on the journey in search of the female sexual response it is essential to know how your entire vagina works. The labia minora, the interior, the perineum, the anus ... But above all, familiarize yourself with the clitoris and learn to work it, because most women do not have vaginal orgasms but clitoris.

THE TONGUE HAS MORE POWER THAN THE SWORD

"If we talk about giving pleasure to a woman, men should speak the language of love: cunnilingus

Of course, oral sex does not have a specific technique either and it will be necessary to rely on success and error until you find the recipe, however, tries to give clues by comparing cunnilingus with Tai Chi by stating that "stillness, balance, pressure and resistance are some of the keys to practicing it."

LADIES FIRST, ALSO FOR ORGASMS

Unlike men, women do not reach a point of ' orgasmic inevitability ', a term that is used to define that moment in which male stimulation reaches a point of no return that leads to orgasm. "In fact, both sexes are so different in this respect that many women claim to lose orgasm just when they are about to reach it, which is really frustrating for them, especially when it happens regularly,"

DON'T MISS A VIBRATOR

It is easier for most women to reach orgasm when a vibrator is used: the mechanical vibration provided by these toys is more intense than any penis, phallus, tongue, fresh produce or other stimuli."

TELL THEM THIS IN BED

Many women commented that they felt more pressure than animation when men interrupted the act with dirty comments. They even explained that they find it hard to verbalize with words if they are enjoying it or not or if they should continue like this or that way. What they like to do in bed is nothing more than moan of pleasure, and it is not pleased that the replica is based on misplaced free insults.

TEST WITH YOUR HANDS

Although many take it as something personal, as if they were doing something wrong, it is perfectly normal and in fact recommended that women take the opportunity to stimulate themselves while practicing sex. In fact, according to the survey data, a negligible 19% said that "almost always" solve the issue themselves; almost half do it "sometimes", and about 10% "want to do it but it is contained".

FEELING SEXY

Every woman needs to feel attractive and desired; For more than 20 years of marriage. But feeling sexy isn't always that easy. Sometimes, we take off our own sensuality. That happens, for example, when we go to bed as if it were another domestic task, because we are ashamed of our bodies, or we are afraid of ridicule if we do "something sexy."

TIME

Yes, we need time!!! Although sometimes that raptured, and wildly wild sex is absolutely exciting; We generally need to devote time to the last game!

For us there must be a favorable environment, with caresses, words and kisses; On the other hand, for them, in most cases, they only need to think about sex to achieve an erection. To us, to get excited, it takes us about 20 minutes ... When the last game is appropriate, vaginal lubrication and the erection of the clitoris is achieved, which is a vital organ in female sexuality.

FEEL PLEASED

A patient who one day told me: "I feel my husband uses me as a toilet!" A lapidary and unfortunate complaint ... She felt, like many other women, that her partner used her to satisfy a physiological function. It entered, moved a little, ejaculated and left. Frightening! No woman can feel well in bed in this way.

What Man Wants?

THEY WANT TO BE TOLD CLEARLY

"Nobody is terrible in bed ", but simply lacks communication skills.

You have to pay attention and be communicative about what you like and what you don't. After all, sexual intercourse is another type of interaction. Isn't it a mistake to eliminate such an essential part of our natural way of communicating with others?

Men, it seems, love to talk and listen to women. They want to know what he wants, how he wants it ... and what he likes to be there with him. Verbal language in bed is fascinating for them

Although some of his fantasies do confess to them to fulfil them, others may still be a little taboo, and either out of shame or fear of rejection they dare not propose them. Discover the unspeakable secrets of men through dirty talking

HAVE CONTROL

Let him take over! They love to take the reins and be the one in control. But they can't deny that the moment you put yourself on top and he lets himself go something that also drives them crazy. That's why role-playing games are perfect for fulfilling these fantasies.

That you are more affectionate

Although this seems one of our desires, it is not so. Men love to be hugged, to look them in the eyes, to give them kisses and tell them how much you love them while making love. Romanticism also attracts them, they are not made of stone

TAKE YOUR TIME

To awaken the desire it takes time, kisses and caresses and that moment of excitement is also significant for them

BE DOMINATED

There are times when all you want is to get under your command, to tie them to bed and let yourself be carried away by the situation. This can be a bit complicated to propose, so there are times that it is better that you simply take the initiative and put yourself in the dominatrix plan. You can get ideas from the following postures to make love tied.

TALK ABOUT YOUR WISHES

Talking about your sexual fantasies while you imagine fulfilling them is something that will plainly put you both to one hundred. Also, while you are in bed in full action, tell you what you like and what is not something that you also love. Encourage him to communicate with you in those moments!

SEE HOW YOU GIVE YOURSELF PLEASURE

Seeing a woman masturbating always drives men crazy, makes her desire increase more. If you want to prolong this moment do not let him touch you, just look until he can no longer, and his excitement is through the clouds.

THE RISQUE LANGUAGE

Men go crazy when you say in your ear all the wicked things that you are going to do in bed. Try to play with him, when you are in public whisper in his ear some wild idea that comes to mind, he will not stop thinking about it!

THE SURPRISES

An erotic dance a set of provocative lingerie, impossible positions taken from the Kamasutra ... Everything that goes out of the routine and fans the flame is welcome. Nor is it necessary to do something complicated but try to make it something original that is not expected. It will drive you crazy!

LOSING CONTROL

Making love slow while romanticism invades the environment they like, but uncontrol ling a little and moving to wild and primitive sex is something they want even more.

COUPLE PORN

That most men watch solo porn is a fact, but it is also that they would like us to see it with them. Think about it! Surely you can get some ideas and put them into practice later ...

SEEING YOURSELF IN FULL ACTION

This plainly more than one would ever recognize, but a mirror on the ceiling or on a wall are great allies for them. They love being in full action!

CHANGE LOCATION

The bedroom and the bed are excellent, but in the end, it ends up being monotonous. Men like risk and change, make love in the kitchen, in the living room, in the bathroom ... Even in a public place! He may be shy, and I do not propose it, but if you have the initiative, we assure you that it will be a fascinating time.

PUT ON A SHOW

Doing a striptease and putting on a whole show is something they love, but on both sides. They are the ones who dance and take off their shirts to the rhythm of the music while they do the erotic movements of Magic Mike, or that it is you who put yourself in plan Demi Moore in the movie Striptease

TURN UP THE VOLUME

An excellent way to let him know that he is on the right track is the groans, for them they are an incentive to try harder and make you reach heaven. Deep breaths and screams of pleasure are welcome, there is nothing more motivating for them!

Seduction and Dirty Talk Before Sex

There is nothing sexier than your partner taking the time and effort to seduce you. We will explore how to dirty talk through sexting and in person, even when you are surrounded by people, as well as how to deal with the often-tricky question of consent without putting out the flame of passion.

How to seduce through text

Sexting is not just for teenagers. It is a great way to add spice to a long-term relationship that maybe began before texting became the go-to method for communication. It is also a very effective way to build anticipation over a long period of time. If you often have trouble becoming aroused and need lots of time and attention, starting early through sexting can really help. Sexts can help you (and your partner) visualize what you are going to do to each other, which will get your sexy parts humming. Arousal starts in the brain, so spending the day thinking about sex will really prime you both. Here is what those types are like:

Reminiscing

This technique is especially good if you are new at dirty talk. Here are some examples of reminiscing sexts:

- "I can't stop thinking about that one time when we..."

- "Remember when you really took charge that one night? I want you do that again."

- "Last night was incredible; it's so hard to focus right now."

- "I was just thinking about that trip we took, and the hotel room had that huge jacuzzi. Remember what we did and how much water splashed out?"

- "I'm figuring out our Christmas plans and I remembered that one year we were trying to be quiet cause your parents were right next door, but it was so hard."

- "Remember a few weekends ago when we just stayed in bed all day? I miss that."

Prompting

It gives them a general guide for where to go and what you are looking for. Paint a picture with your words to get them excited, like so:

- "I just got out of the shower and I'm dripping wet right now. Can you guess what I'm thinking about?"

- "When you get home, I'm going to be waiting in the bedroom. What do you do first?"

- "I'm so bored at work right now, and I'm getting hard/wet thinking about you. What are you wearing?"

- "Just woke up from a bad dream, and I'm scared. Any idea what would make me feel better?"

- "I ate the rest of the ice cream you were saving for tonight. How are you going to punish me?"

Teasing

Teasing keeps things light and fun, but still sexy. Here are some examples:

- "When you come home, I've got a surprise for you."

- "I'm thinking about you and touching myself. I bet you wish you were home right now."

- "Can you guess what I'm thinking about?"

- "I had a hot dream last night, and it gave me some ideas."

- "I just got out of a meeting, but I couldn't stop thinking about you. I hope my boss didn't notice."

- "I should be cleaning cause the house is so dirty, but I'm thinking about something else that's dirty."

- "If you aren't busy tonight, I have a good idea for how to spend the evening."

Foreshadowing

It can be vague or specific, depending on your comfort level.

- "Tonight, I'm going to take it really slow and make you beg for it."

- "The things I have in mind for us tonight are going to blow your mind."

- "The minute you get home, I'm getting on my knees for you."

- "You're going to scream my name tonight."

- "It's going to be so intense; you're not going to be able to move after I'm done with you."

- "I'm going to make you cum so hard."

Other sexting tips

What are some general sexting tips that can keep you safe from embarrassment?

Send sexts when you know your partner is not busy

There is nothing quite as exciting as a naughty text when you are sitting bored at work or on a lonely night alone, but if you're walking into a meeting or with your family, it can be super awkward.

Be careful when sending pics

When sending not-safe-for-work pics, make sure it is not going to pop up on your partner's lock screen where anyone who glances over can see it. You can keep it hidden by writing some text, hitting return a few times, and then adding the photo. If you and your partner are planning on sexting in the future, it is a good idea to adjust both phones.

Have fun with emojis

Did you know you can dirty talk just using emojis? These cute little icons can represent things that are more hot than cute, and it can be a fun way to communicate with your partner without using words.

Like a good old-fashioned letter?
We talked about sexting, but that is not the only way you can employ dirty talk through writing. A lot of people really love messages they can hold in their hands. Taking the effort to sit down and write something by hand shows your partner you really care and are paying attention to what turns them on. Post-its can be like sexts because they are so short, but what if you want your special letter to really stand out? Here are some ideas on how to write a good erotic love letter:

Describe your partner using all your senses
When you are writing your letter, you can write about whatever you want, like a memory. Think about what you remember, like how they moved, the sound of their voice, and even what they smelled like.

Be choosy about your words
Here are some words to consider:

- Tremble ("Your touch makes me tremble.")

- Linger ("I want to take my time with you, lingering on your lips.")

- Tingle ("When you kiss me, I can feel my pussy tingle.")

- Savor ("I want to savor every moment.")

- Ruthless ("I love it when you're ruthless with me, taking me as your own.")

- Naughty ("That little naughty smile of yours never fails to turn me on.")

- Luscious ("I want to eat you like a luscious peach.")

- Delicious ("Tasting your lips, your skin, you're delicious.")

- Inviting ("When you pull me close, inviting me inside, I'm overwhelmed.")

Make it emotional and personal

A handwritten letter is the perfect opportunity to bring out the emotional big guns as well as the erotic ones. Just remember to let them know your deeper feelings, as well.

Dirty talking in public

You are out on the town with your partner and hoping that the evening takes a sexy turn. You do not have to wait until you are back at home to start talking dirty. Here are some examples of what to whisper in your lover's ear, both subtle and not-at-all subtle:

- "I wish we could be alone right now."

- "I'm having a really hard time not touching you."

- "You look so sexy in that outfit, but I can't wait to rip it off you."

- "Can you guess what I'm thinking about right now?"

- "Do you think anyone would care if we went home early?"

- "When we get home, the first thing I'm going to do is push you against the wall and kiss you."

- "That dinner was amazing, but I think I'm hungry for something else now."

- "If the people around me could read my mind, they would be so embarrassed."

- "I'm really glad no one here can read my mind."

Locations for dirty talk

Here are some ideas that range from very safe to very risky:

- In a loud nightclub

- In a movie theater

- At a concert

- At a friend's house when they leave the room

- At the family barbecue

- At a play

- At a wedding ceremony/reception

- Waiting in line at the grocery store

- In an airplane

- In a taxi/Uber

- At dinner in a quiet restaurant

- Waiting for a train/subway

- At church

Finding your seductive voice

When dirty talking, your tone of voice is often even more important than the actual words you are saying. The brain is very sensitive to sound, which is why heavy breathing, moaning, and other noises that are not words can be very arousing. Here are some tips on how to make your voice more seductive:

Go deep

Voices with a deeper register give the impression of calmness and confidence. This is true in general, not just with sex, which is why people with deep voices are often taken more seriously than those with higher pitches. Going higher creates a feeling of anxiety or insecurity.

Go low

Shouting and screaming have their place in sex, but when it comes to seduction, going soft is best. Speaking quietly is much more intimate since your partner must pay close attention to your words, and maybe even lean in. Dirty talk that is so quiet only two people can hear is one of the most special intimate experiences.

Practice

There are specific vocal techniques you can do to build your sexiest voice. For going deeper, hum from high to low notes while paying attention to the feelings each pitch produces in your body. When you speak and lower your voice, see how those feelings line up. For softening your voice, experiment with sexy phrases, raising and lowering the volume to find out what sounds and feels best. Best of all, the more you practice, the more comfortable you will be, and that will translate into confidence. You will feel sexier and your voice will reflect that.

Dirty talk and consent

There is a misconception that asking for consent is an unsexy thing, but when you use dirty talk, it is extremely sexy. Finding out what your partner is up for and taking the time to really woo them is what good seduction is all about. Here are some ideas on how to sexily ask for consent before things really get going:

- "Would you like to move things to the bedroom?"

- "Can I help you with that?"

- "Is it okay if I take off your shirt/bra/pants/panties/etc.?"

- "Is it okay if I kiss you here (name body part)?"

- "Do you want me to keep going?"

- "Do you want me to go down on you?"

- "Is it okay if I put my hands here (name body part)?"

- "Does this feel good?"

- "Do you like it when I... (touch you here, put my mouth on this body part, take you from behind, ride you really hard, etc.)."

- "Tell me exactly what to do to you."

- "I'm all yours, tell me what you want me to do to you."

Main takeaways

Sexting is a great way to build tension and anticipation. There are four ways to dirty talk through text: remembering past sexual memories, asking questions, teasing, and hinting at the show to come. Always be careful when sexting and sending pics, since phones are not always super secure or someone else might glance at the screen at the wrong time. Sprinkling good old' fashioned love letters with dirty talk is both sexy and romantic. Dirty talk in public, whether you keep it subtle or more provocative, gets foreplay started early. You can improve your bedroom voice through tricks like deepening your pitch and playing with your volume. Unlike what many might think, getting consent is a great opportunity for white-hot dirty talk.

Dirty Talk during the Sex

Talking dirty during sex can turn all your fantasies into reality. There is so much to comment/say during sex that you should let your imagination and mouth run wild with all kinds of ideas that pop into your mind. You can give your partner directions of how and what you want him to do to you, what kind of things you want to do to him, describe the way it feels having sex with him, tell him how you want him to call you, give him compliments and encourage him. There are plenty of options to dirty talk about! And do not forget about moaning and groaning. Sometimes it might be difficult to say the lines due to the shortness of breath during sex. However, it is very sexy to say a dirty line, panting.

I will do you at present; do you need it in your pussy or your rear end?

This kind of definitive proclamation characterizes which individual is prevailing in that specific circumstance shows that the partner despite everything has a specific measure of through and through freedom during the activities to come.

I need to screw you.

This is like one of our articulations, in any case, this shows you are assuming responsibility for the circumstance; you are the predominant, and it has the entirety of the suggestions that are related with this specific idea.

Recall how you made me shout a week ago? Do it once more.

The thought that you have been (persistently) considering that specific demonstration all week, or whatever variety of time (day, and so on.) you include into this specific stating, shows the amount you really appreciated it, yet in addition that you haven't had the option to get them off your psyche.

That feels unimaginable; kindly do not stop.

Although it might appear to be a manageable expression, it completes a few things. In the first place, it gives approval that your partner is accomplishing something so incredibly, right, and second, by saying if it is not too much trouble it places them in charge of the circumstance.

Much the same as that.

With these three little words, you are indicating that you like what is being done to you, and in doing as such, are furnishing them with motivating force to continue onward.

Try not to stop.

You are revealing to them that they are doing something right and that they should proceed. This likewise serves to bring explicit thoughtfulness regarding a specific activity that you particularly appreciate, guaranteeing that it will happen again later.

Harder.

Many folks, regardless of whether subliminally or not, will treat a young lady like she's going to break, and this shows you're truly into it, that you won't break, and that you can take whatever they can hand out. This separates specific outlook, regardless of whether they understand that it is available, and all things considered, the more crude and carnal sides will come out in both of you, turning something well-known into something unquestionably increasingly basic.

Turnover.

The more drawn out between the words being expressed, the activity being performed, and the following move is made, the almost certain degree of excitement will ascend to an extraordinary extent.

It turns me on so much when you nail me down.

Individuals need to realize that they are wanted; by revealing to them an activity that makes you want them more, you are giving a certainty help, however likewise giving them that you do not need the relationship to end.

I love the inclination you within me.

This shows your partner that you are not faking it; you need them, you love the wonderful way they feel, you cannot envision anything superior to that at that point. It is everything that you need.

I do not think there is anything more sweltering than watching your face when you come.

This shows giving your partner delight gives you extraordinary joy consequently; with it additionally comes a feeling of achievement and fulfillment at an occupation well done.

Doggie style feels unbelievable with you.

Any position can be embedded toward the start of this specific expression, achieving a few things; first, you are complimenting them by referencing them in particular, and second, you are mentioning to them what position you truly preferred out of anyway numerous you may have happened to experience that round.

There is something so madly hot about nailing you down.

This shows your partner that the very demonstration of playing out specific follows up on them, to them, or for them, is a staggeringly sexual encounter for you, further approving that you need to be there with them at that time.

Nobody has ever constructed me come as hard as you do.

While truly, this is a similar explanation, and you will commonly need to remain away from these, the same number of similar explanations won't come out the way they are expected, this serves to expand your partner's sense of self a considerable amount by telling them that they are the best you have had, which thusly suggests that you need to keep getting precisely what they need to provide for you.

You like it when I spread my legs for you and take you in, isn't that right?

To talk about the activities that are happening, you are giving a soundtrack for the visuals that are going on before your partner's face, expanding their want twofold.

I need to suck your dick until you come.

Straightforward, and great on the off chance that you love giving head. It is rarely turned down, and to show the activity and the craving to do as such independently truly improves the demonstration itself. Get happiness out of the way that you are accomplishing something you appreciate, and happiness from the certainty that your partner is truly having a good time and go from that point.

Jump on top.

Like advising your partner to turn over, instructing them to jump on top gives a wide range of pictures, and various potential approaches to do as such; with both partners envisioning the various ways this could occur, it truly helps the sensations.

I need you to ride me hard.

The intensity of mentioning to your partner what you need to occur straight away, what you need to do straightaway, or what you need them to do straightaway, goes about as a groundbreaking love potion, giving them that you want them, which thus expands your longing as you see their longing increment.

Is it true that you are my insidious little bitch?

This will rely upon if your partner approves of being known as a bitch, yet when utilized right now, becomes an affectionate nickname, and if the appropriate response given is truly, extra joy would then be able to be given to them as an award for being "acceptable."

I love screwing you.

There is no less difficult approach to tell somebody how much delight you escape being as one, in the scriptural sense, with them, and the suggestion is that you wish to keep doing as such, appearing in another way that you will near wish to keep doing as such, appearing in another way that you will be near for whatever length of time that you are capable.

I love sucking your rooster, and I am going to lick you clean.

Mentioning to your partner what you need to do, and being so unequivocal about the demonstration can be done in the demonstration itself, investigate what will occur straightaway, causing a wide range of lovely mental pictures and expanding their want and expectation of what is to come exponentially.

I love the delightful way huge your rooster gets, how much this turns me on.

This offers another approach to stroke a man's sense of self, and fills in as not just approval, yet, helps fearlessness immensely; the expanded certainty level will make them bound to do different things that they may have been going back and forth about doing beforehand.

The sounds you make me insane.

This expression serves to urge your partner to make more clamor, however, guarantees them that they are not making any strange or off-putting commotions, facilitating any stress or trepidation they may have had about the sounds that were coming out of their mouths.

I am going to screw you until you cannot walk.

The inalienable foulness gave by this announcement can make your partner get their breath, for all that it infers, and all the various situations that can be envisioned off these couple of straightforward words.

I am so screwing wet.

Another expression that shows your partner the amount you want them explicitly, which thus gets them significantly more smoking, and accordingly, the cycle proceeds. You appear to them that they are the person who matters, and nobody else, and that your longing is a direct aftereffect of their specific activities.

Good Gracious, Fuck.

At times intelligent words simply do not exist, and all things considered, this old backup will continuously work to show that you are only this side of beginning to lose total and all out coherency because of whatever it is they are doing.

It is hard to believe, but it is true, ride me.

It's one thing to be prodded, it's very another to be advised to keep on prodding yourself, and the rush that comes from being advised to do as such, however, to utilize your partner's hand to do so significantly builds the impact.

Take it.

Advising your partner to take all that you have as you increment the power of your activity is an incredible inclination, a basic inclination, which serves to draw out the marginally carnal side in people and serves to heighten the sensations themselves as they react back, asking, requesting, asking for all that you're willing to give.

Screw me. At the present time.

Another genuine sense of self-promoter, demonstrating that regardless, any further postponement, even that of a subsequent will be extremely long, and you can't pause, want nothing more, than to screw them without even a second's pause, paying little heed to where you are, or who might be around.

I need you to utilize me as your toy throughout the night.

Again, this expressing not just shows that you are surrendering control to your partner, yet in addition shows the degree of trust that you have in your partner; that they will make it a commonly helpful and commonly charming experience, as restricted to leaving one gathering feeling like they're being utilized.

Top me off with your enormous dick; screw my tight cunt.

Not exclusively does this specific manner of expression fill in as a self-image help for both of you, it likewise gives express depictions that will serve to energize the two partners and upgrade the general understanding.

You can have me any way you need me.

This is another expression that can be utilized to surrender control to your partner and show that you have the most extreme trust in them, that they won't hurt you, or misuse you in any capacity, and that they will guarantee that both of you have an awesome time.

Spread your legs for me.

This direction shows who will be the prevailing party for this specific time, or through the course of the accompanying explicit activities, requesting that they open to you, genuinely, yet intellectually also. It guarantees that both partners are in that spot where the moves are making place, rather than lost in their own heads.

Quicker!

This shows you are drawing nearer and closer to detonating, and the closer you get, the more contact you need, which will thusly make them get their pace because of expanded excitement from hearing this one straightforward word come out of your mouth.

100 Dirty Talk Examples

The dirty talk applies to either gender or can be a fun way to spice up your sex life. If you are just getting started, aim for the milder phrases, but feel free to add in your own wording or move on to the hotter phrases as you feel ready.

You can use these different ideas for sexy talk to create your own hot lines, as well. The trick here is to get creative. Just use what is listed below as inspiration.

Mild Dirty Talk

I want you.

You are so hot/sexy.

I love every inch of your body.

We fit so perfectly together.

You need to take those clothes off right now.

You turn me on/make me horny.

The way you smell/look/taste/feel drives me wild.

You can stay, but the clothes got to go.

We really should be filming this.

You are the best lay I have ever had.

Making you horny is one of my favorite things to do.

I love how you smell/taste/feel.

You make me feel so good.

Tease me until I am begging for it.

You better be naked when I get home.

God, I love how you feel against me.

Our bodies were made for each other. They fit perfectly.

I am going to make you feel so good.

The way you walk/cook/talk turns me on so much.

I just want to do this forever.

I could lie here/cuddle you forever like this.

You have no idea how much you/your body turn(s) me on.

You are amazing.

You taste like _____.

You drive me crazy when you _____.

Your _____ is/are so beautiful.

Shut up and just kiss me.

I am making the rules/in control tonight.

Cancel everything you planned tonight. Tonight, you are mine.

As you wish.

You make me feel so good.

Oh baby, you are the best.

Come make love to me. I need you.

How did I get so lucky?

Oh, god, that feels so good!

You are going to make me cum already.

That is perfect, keep it up.

Tell me you are mine.

I want to explore every nook and cranny of your body.

I cannot handle not being able to touch you.

I never knew I could want someone this much.

Your lips are irresistible.

Do you even realize what you do to me?

I will do whatever you want, just tell me when and where.

I love to feel the heat of your body on my skin.

Dirty Talk

Where do you want me to make you cum?

You look good in that outfit. Now take it off.

I have not been this horny since I first discovered masturbating.

Bite me right there.

I love making/watching you cum.

Cumming together is the best part.

I need a good fuck right now, you up for it.

I want to cum for you so hard.

You are the hottest fuck ever.

You feel so sexy to me.

How bad do you want to cum for me?

I have been naughty; you better give me a spanking.

Everything you do with your tongue is incredible.

You have been bad and now you are going to get a spanking.

I have never gotten so turned on just by kissing someone.

You can have me any way you want right now.

Oh yes, keep doing that!

No one has ever turned me on like you do.

Do not stop!

You can relax, I am going to do all the work this time/tonight.

I can still smell you on me and it is wonderful.

I am coming.

I am so horny, get over here and make me cum.

I cannot wait to taste you.

I want your hands on me right now.

Eye contact with you is all the foreplay I need.

Cum for me, baby.

You are a sex fantasy come to life.

I want your lips on every part of my body.

You are so sexy when you cum.

Tell me all the dirty things you want to do to me.

I am trying to listen to you, but you are just too damn sexy.

I cannot stop thinking about your taste on my tongue.

I am going to rip those clothes off you and throw you on the bed.

I am addicted to your body against mine.

I want to make you scream in pleasure.

Keep this up and I am going to fucking explode.

I always get what I want, and I want you.

You make me want to be very, very bad.

Keep the lights on so I can see you while we fuck.

Filthy Phrases

I am going to fuck you so hard we wake the neighbors.

Let us fuck so hard we break the bed.

Let us go to the movies and screw our brains out in the back row.

I do not care if someone hears, I am too horny to wait.

Get ready, I am going to fuck your brains out.

Fuck me like you paid for it.

Let us do it like we are auditioning for a porn movie.

Let us fuck until we pass out.

I want to fuck you in front of the mirror.

You are so fucking sexy in that position.

Tell me how much you want me to fuck you.

Do not make a sound until I say you can, or I will stop fucking you until you're quiet again.

This is going to be the filthiest night of your life.

Do not you dare cum until I say you can.

I am going to make you cum so hard the whole street will know my name.

Dirty Talk Variations

Dirty talk does not have to be limited to face-to-face interactions. In the world of cutting-edge technology, it is possible to implement dirty talk in emailing, texting (sexting), handwritten notes/letters, phone sex and other digital means of communication. When your partner reads a sexy note from you, they cannot stop their imagination getting carried away. Love letters have been around for centuries, and there is something extra special about reading saucy words or hearing them.

Another advantage to written sex talk is the lack of pressure to immediately respond. The recipient can take their time with a well thought out seductive response.

Phone sex or even skype are both very good alternatives to the real thing when you are away from one another. You can also have some fun with imaginative, and fun picture messages.

Emails

Emailing might seem a little formal, but it can be sexy too! One important thing to keep in mind is: always check who you are sending your email to before you click 'send'. You do not want it to be your co-worker, or worse, your boss.

- Seductive. "I know you are busy at work, but I just wanted to let you know that I'm thinking about last night."

- Seductive. "I can't forget that last kiss you gave me. I want more!!"

- Saucy. "When you get this message, imagine me kissing your abs and going lower and lower."

- Saucy. "I've been thinking about you all day long. I'm getting so wet, just responding to you."

- Filthy. "I've been typing this message for hours, thinking about you and fingering myself."

- Filthy. "When you get home, we are going to fuck like we are the only people left on earth."

Texting (sexting)

This a less formal way of talking dirty to your partner through digital means as we always have our phones on us. The key rule of dirty talk texting is to respond as quickly as possible and not let your partner hanging. When the sexual tension builds up, you do not want to lose it and start all over again. Just be provocative, creative and dig deep in your sexual fantasies to express the strongest desires toward your partner.

- Seductive. "I can't stop thinking about your muscular chest."

- Seductive. "I'm sucking on a popsicle right now. Just FYI."

- Seductive. "I want you here. Right now. Naked."

- Saucy. "I've just come out of the shower, and I was thinking about you in it."

- Saucy. "What would you do to me if I was standing naked in front of you now?"

- Saucy. "You know what? I woke up wet this morning. Guess who I was dreaming about?"

- Filthy. "I don't know how to tell you this, so I'm just going to write it down: I want you to bang me so hard I can barely move."

- Filthy. "If only you could feel how wet I am right now..."

- Filthy. "I can't help but touch my pussy when I think about you."

Handwritten notes/letters

Handwritten notes and letters are special and unique because you put much more effort and passion into them. They are romantic, and yet can be extremely hot. If you do it right, your man will hold this piece of paper you wrote on, thinking about your hand touching it. However, it is important to note a letter, or a note may get into the wrong hands. Of course, you do not want anybody to read the correspondence between you and your partner, but the mere existence of such a risk enhances sexual arousal.

You can stash a note in your partner's bag where you know they will find it and tell them what you want to do to them tonight or it can be more immediate. You can leave a note when you are around and wait for them to read it and find you. Be creative!

- Seductive. "I wish you could just hold me in your strong arms all day long."

- Seductive. "I can't wait to show you what I'm wearing. You're going to love it!"

- Saucy. "You may notice it by my handwriting, but I'm touching myself as I write this."

- Saucy. "I'm not going to write a script of how I want you to make love to me tonight, but I'm going to say this: I want it to be hotter than the hottest scene in 50 Shades of Grey."

- Filthy. "I want you to fuck me hard. Tonight."

- Filthy. "I'm lying naked on the bed upstairs. I want you to cum all over me right now."

Phone sex

It is no secret that you can make your man aroused just with the sound of your voice. It is totally up to you what kind of voice to use: slow, seductive, provocative, fast, and aggressive, or mix it all up. Just speak your mind and run wild with the idea of bringing pleasure to both you and your partner without touching and seeing one another. Ask him what he is wearing, tell him how much you want him right now. Be more precise when describing the way, you feel and the things that you would love to do to him right now. Do not forget to moan and groan. That is probably the key to success during phone sex. Try to make phone sex as close to real sex as possibly can.

- Seductive. "I'm wearing these sexy stockings I told you about."

- Seductive. "I'm not wearing any underwear right now."

- Seductive. "Your voice makes my whole body tremble with ecstasy."

- Saucy. "Talking to you right now is making me horny."

- Saucy. "I have to confess; I can't talk to you without touching myself."

- Saucy. "I want you to tell me how you imagine me as you play with your penis."

- Filthy. "I want you to take your cock and jerk off to the sound of my moaning, baby."

- Filthy. "Oh... My sheets are so wet with my cum right now."

- Filthy. "I want to feel your cock inside my pussy so badly now. The distance makes me go crazy."

What to Say?

Erotic Noises

Most everyone is comfortable with erotic noises and it is a very good place to start. They are as natural as making a deep exhaled sigh as you relax down into a hot bubble bath or when you are getting a massage. Mmmmmmm, Ooooooh, Ahhhhhh, Yeeesssss, moaning, groaning, sighs, and breathy exhales are normal and instinctive when something feels so very, very good.

Nice Phrases

Nice phrases are simple, yet effective, and step two to the process. Nice phrases are an easy way to dip your toes in the water of dirty talk and will add a little excitement to your romp.

- Yes, right there!

- Oh yeah, that is nice. You smell wonderful.

- That feels so good! Touch me here.

- I am so happy to be wrapped up here with you. Your mouth feels amazing.

- I feel so safe in your arms. I am so loving this!

- I have been thinking about doing this to you all day long.

Poetic Phrases

Classical, Old English, Medieval and Poetic speech used to titillate your partner. While not the type of speech you hear every day, some people prefer a more timeless or poetic speech between them and their partner. Something they see as a little more creative and less commonly used that has meaning just between the two of them.

Some examples of these are:

- Your deep valley is so alluring.

- You charm and entice me like no other. You are my knight – take me.

- Those dewy mounds of yours delight my tongue. Your body is my velvet canvas

- My ocean wants to crash onto your beach. I am drunk on your fragrance and affection

Asian Poetic Phrases

Some examples of Asian/poetic words for describing your lover's body are:

HERS

- Golden Crevice, Honey Pot, Precious Gateway,

- Pleasure Field of Heaven, Enchanted Garden,

- Cinnabar Grotto, Flower Heart, Jade Gate,

- Celestial Palace, The Precious Pearl

HIS

- Crimson Bird, Celestial Dragon,

- Mushroom of Immortality, Healing Scepter,

- Jade Stalk, Jade Stem and Rainbow Serpent

Hot Phrases!!

Once you have mastered some erotic sounds you will feel a little more comfortable vocalizing with your mate. Try adding some of these Hot Phrases, but feel free to change up the 'body part' words with what you are most comfortable with. Below are some examples of Hot Phrases:

- Your pussy tastes so sweet.

- My panties get wet just thinking about what you are going to do to me.

- I want your thick meat!!

- I want to be so satisfied, that everyone who sees me tomorrow will know why I am still smiling.

- I adore those soft breasts.

- Oh baby, I want to cum all over you.

- Who makes that cock so hard, cowboy?

- Let me suck on those nipples.

- I want to fuck you all night long. Mmmmm, harder, do not stop!! Can you feel how wet you get me?

- Oh yeah, that is it, do not you dare stop fucking me. You like banging this slick pussy, don't you?

- Put me on my knees and bang me till I cum all over your dick. Do not stop fucking me until I beg you!

- Your cunt feels so hot on my cock.

- You are making my dick head swell so big. I want to lick that dick like a lollipop.

- I love pumping that moist pussy. Man, you are so tight, so delightful.

- I have been thinking about fucking you all day.

- You are so hot – I am going to fill you with my juice. I love to feel that hot cock inside me.

- Your prick tastes so good. I want more. Please give me more of your fat rod.

Hardcore Phrases

Edgy, raw and being totally frank about what it is that you want, hard core phrases convey just that. Not for the timid and not the first thing you should throw at your partner during your first ever encounter with 'dirty talk'. Consider this the ultimate walk on the wild side compared to the basic 'tamer' talk we just read.

Many couples will never make it to this level. And that is ok. It is not some video game where the higher you go, the better. It is really all about your partner. If you find that hardcore phrases turn both of you on, then go for it. But if it ruins the lovemaking experience for your beloved, do not go there. Take it down a notch or two. We are all a little bit different in what rocks our world.

Here are some examples of hardcore phrases:

- My throbbing cock wants to plunge in your dripping wet pussy. I want your fat dig to spew cum all up inside me.

- Whip it out and cum all over my tits!

- Watch me while I am sucking your balls and licking the underside of that gorgeous cock of yours!

- Get on your knees and suck my rod dry.

- Do you want to spank my ass while you are grinding me from behind? Tell me you want to swallow my load!!

- I am going to let you eat me after you fuck me for a few minutes first. Do you want me to deep throat that cock of yours, baby?

- Watch me tilt my head back and lick my juices off that rock hard piece of meat!

- Sit on my face lover.

- My tongue wants to be so deep in that wet, sweet hole. I am going to fuck that dripping wet pussy all night.

"I Want" Phrases

To get the communication rolling, these "I WANT" phrases are often easier to just begin with for couples. Telling your lover what it is you "want".

For example:

- I want to eat your pussy till you scream out and orgasm.

- I want to flip you over and ride your doggy style.

- I want to put your dick right here between my tits.

- I want you to pull my hair while I am on my hands and knees. I want you to slide your meaty cock deep into my cunt.

- I want you to climb on top of me.

- I want you to throw my legs up over your shoulders. I want you in me deeper.

- I want to watch you stroke yourself.

- I want you to show me how you like it, baby.

- I want you to teach me how to stroke it the way you like it.

- I want you to squat above my hard dick and pump up and down on it like a piston.

- I want you to explode so deep in my hot snatch.

Substituting "I NEED" or "WILL YOU" works with all these phrases, so feel free to change it up.

"Play By Play"

If you are at a loss for words, you can do "play by play" dirty talk. Simply describe what is taking place as you are doing it:

- Oh yeah, you are sucking on my nipples and it is getting me so very wet. I am fingering your dripping, wet pussy.

- I am so turned on by that precum dripping off the head of your dick.

- You have got your hand wrapped around my hot cock and it feels so nice. I am going to climb on top of you and ride you, cowboy.

- I am licking you from head to toe, baby – you are so tasty. I am going to lift my legs so you can get a better view.

- I can see your dripping cock sliding in and out of me from this position and it is getting me even wetter!

- Oh yeah, here it comes, I am cumming baby!! I am going to explode in that pussy.

Asking Questions

- How hard does that dick feel inside of you?

- Do you like the way my tongue feels on your clit? Do you like it slow and easy, or fast and hard?

- How sloppy do you want it to sound when I am sucking on that cock? Would you like to hold my head and control the rhythm?

- Do you feel my dick getting harder inside of you, girl?

- Maybe you like the way I dart it in and out of your hot, dripping hole? How about I stick a finger inside, would you like that honey?

- Do you like the way my tits bounce around when you are giving it to me like that?

- Can I run my fingernails lightly over your scrotum when you get close to shooting off inside of me?

- How fast do you want me to pump that pussy? Do you like it when I grind on that pole?

Using Text to Talk Dirty

Sexting is like foreplay before foreplay. If you do it in the right way, it can be so tantalizing. I will share secrets to some seriously effective sexting.

Just like dirty talk on the phone, in person, and during sex, you can ease into sexting by simply letting them know how they make you feel and what you want them to do to you. Do not get too dirty too soon. In most cases, some say do not sext unless you have already had sex. If you have not already been intimate, instigating via cell phone can be risky. Three percent of adults in the U.S. have forwarded along sexts they received to others. You do not want to be one of the victims of forwarded sexts especially sexts that include suggestive pictures.

The most popular time to send texts is between 10 am and noon on Tuesdays.

The key to sending a sexy text message is to keep it interesting and subtle. No need to go overboard with it. It is pre-foreplay which means it is not an act of sex itself but just a hint of sexual explicitness. In the context of sexting, less is always more. The main purpose is to keep your partner wondering about your sexual appetite and fantasies. Having said that, sexting is very sexual in its own way; there might not be a physical touch involved in it, but it is like sex for the mind. With sexting, you are letting your partner know that you are ready for the act and what your fantasies are, meaning what all you expect from your partner during sex. It broadens the sexual boundaries between you and your partner and yields the spice in your relationship.

The Dream Text

One effective way to gage if you partner likes sexting or is ready for you to sexting is to use "The Dream Text". The text goes something like "I just had a wild dream last night and you were in it." If he/she knows where you are going with it, he/she can either stop you or reinforce you. If he/she asks, "Tell me more" you can respond by saying "It was R rated" or "It was definitely X rated." Now you have made sure that they know where you are going, and you'll be able to see if they respond positively so you can keep going with the conversation by text.

Examples of sexting messages

- "I'm imagining you're with me right now."

- "I can't stop thinking about you. I would so love to feel your lips on mine."

- "I want you next to me so bad right now."

- "I want to feel your body pressed up against me."

- "If only you could see what I'm wearing right now."

- "Damn it's hard getting any work done today, I can't top thinking about your (sex, body, face etc.)"

- "Remember when you made me cum twice in a row? I can't stop thinking about it." (Activating memories will stimulate an additional part of your lover's brain)

- What are you wearing right now?

- Are you alone tonight? Want to play a game?

- I was thinking about you in the shower today.

- I will see you in a while. I have got a sexy surprise for you.

- What do you want me to wear later tonight?

- You and me, in a nice hotel tonight?

- When you are around, everything starts throbbing and it is not just my heart I am talking about.

- If you are tired, then I can give you a massage tonight. Let me know where you want my hands to work the most.

- Want to scream tonight? Come by my place.

- You know how to push the right buttons.

- Next time we see each other, I am going to show you what love is.

- I do not need to watch porn anymore. One look at your sexy body keeps me going.

- Why are your keeping me starved?

- Next time when I am around you, wear something that keeps me guessing.

- I am feeling very restless. Would you please come by and tie me up tonight? I will let you do whatever you want to do with me.

- I will be your prisoner tonight.

- Can I have my way with you?

- If you could read my mind, you would start feeling really shy around me.

- How can you turn me on so much just by looking at me?

- What are your plans with me later tonight?

- Let me be a part of your favorite fantasy.

- I had a dream of you last night; you were mostly naked in it.

- I can probably reach climax just by staring at your ass.

- I got a whole new way to love you. Want to know what?

- How about chocolate syrup all over?

- What were you thinking yesterday when your hands were all over me?

- I want to be naughty with you in the office.

- I have got a BIG surprise for you. It is in my pants and it will BLOW your mind.

- I feel wasted just by looking at your pictures.

- It gives me goose bumps just by thinking what I will do to your body.

- Are you ready to go all night?

- Did you tell me to 'come and get it' with your eyes last night?

- My favorite thing on a dessert is whipped cream. Would you let me put it on you?

- I know what you want, and I think I am ready.

- Just to let you know, I am a rider.

- I have read some sexy things on the internet. Would you let me try it on you?

- Why am I horny and you are so far away?

- I think I need a doctor for this little love disease that I got. Would you please examine me from top to bottom?

- I have got a new move. Will you let me show it to you later?

- I have heard that you should not fight it if you like it.

- You left me turned on last night.

- Can you please save some energy for later, after you finish your gym? I have got a task for you.

- I will let you frisk me if you will come and see me in next half an hour.

- I will let you see mine if I will get to see yours.

- Want to play tonight?

- I have been thinking about some seriously racy stuff about you today.

- You can look at it, but you cannot touch it, YET.

- Let us skip dinner tonight and eat something else.

- We should stay in a hotel tonight. I am not sure if my neighbors would appreciate all the pounding noise and screaming.

- I will follow you everywhere if you will let me COME with you.

- Your ass drives me mad.

- Your dessert is HOT and READY for you.

- Do you know if there is a way that I can resist those juicy lips of yours?

- Why can't I take your wet kisses out of my mind?

- How will I be able to contain myself when I know that you are in the shower right now?

- Did you think about me when you were in the bath/shower today?

- Just the smell of you gives me shivers.

- I am laying out right now in the sun.

- I just looked at your picture on my phone and you have sent my dial on high.

- Let us get dirty tonight and wash it off each other in the shower later.

- I am so into you. I want to be in you.

- I am thirsty for you, when can I see you?

- I just want to feel you on me.

- Would you send me some pictures? Pictures you have not sent to anybody else.

- Tonight, in the club we will have our own dancing session, in a dark corner.

- It is hot today; I think I am going to take my all my clothes off and just lay in my bed.

- I am craving you.

- You are so good to me. I am thinking of pleasing you all night tonight.

- I am sending you this text with one hand; my other hand is busy.

- Come and join me.

- You are going to be really exhausted by the end of the night tonight.

- I want to serve you.

- I want to kiss you so bad, all over.

- I want to feel your strong grip on me.

- All we are going to do tonight is tease each other. Are you ready for the torture?

- I am tired of sending you texts or speaking on phone. Why do not you come here and sit on the top of me?

- How did you feel when I groped you in a public place last night in my dream?

- I am dripping with love and desire for you.

- Come on and soak me dry with that mouth of yours.

- I need you right now.

- I get so turned on just thinking about the last time we made love.

- I feel so weak and turned on when I am next to you.

- I want to give you the best oral sex you have ever had.

- I want you to slowly kiss me from my lips, down my neck, down my stomach, all the way down my body

- "I've been fantasizing about taking you like this for a long time."

- When it comes to sexting, most importantly, keep it real.

Texting Photos:

They say a picture's worth a thousand words. So, instead of a full on nude shot or crotch shot, send something visually suggestive. Take a shot of your cleavage, your chest, or a peak of your abs. Really, anything can be sexy just make sure you use proper light and your room looks clean.

Never send pictures of you naked with your face. You do not want to be one of those scary stories of leaked pictures. You make yourself way more mysterious and interesting if you give yourself something to look forward to. Even if you are horny, tame it down a bit. You can talk naughty and flirty but do not get too dirty too soon.

Whether you like something, or you do not, tell your partner. Positive reinforcement can be just what your partner needs to keep the conversation going. (Ex. Ohhh yeah, you are driving me crazy over here, keep it coming).

Do not say "OMG you are making me so wet/hard." It totally kills the vibe. If you want to sound like a sexual grown up, then talk the talk. Do not use too many emojis. The only thing that has the flirty charm is the ;). When it comes to sexting, keep it real. Do not say anything you would not do in person. It will only create complications. Say only what is in your heart and mind. The most important thing to remember when it comes to sexting is to gage where your lover is at and make sure they are reciprocating, and it is a balanced back and forth.

When you are into a heavy sexting conversation, in order to escalate it you want to get him/her on the phone. If you are not comfortable with that, you can say "Okay enough of this I'm coming over" or "I can't take it anymore I need to see you tonight."

General Rules

Not everyone is comfortable with dirty talk. It is crucial to understand people's boundaries and respect them. It is also vital to let your partner know and respect your boundaries. Even if you both agree to spice up your bedroom experience with naughty talks and chitchats, it is necessary to define what is comfortable for you both and want is off-limits.

This will help you and your partner to define exactly how filthy you want to get with words. But before then, let us examine what makes up the contents of naughty phrases.

The Contents of Your Naughty Phrases

Talking dirty does not necessarily mean spewing a string of vulgar words. Instead, it is using words in ways that say, "I am unashamed to let my true feelings show." Of course, a lot of the times curse words or bad language allows us to create the impact we want. But that does not mean everything that comes out of your mouth in the form of dirty talk must be crude. For example, "I can't wait to stroke, kiss, suck, and choke on your huge penis." Or, "I want to nibble on your hard nipples and bury my face between your warm thighs." These phrases may not contain curse words but whispering them in your partner's ear can get them sexually aroused in no time. Remember that the goal is to heighten sexual arousal and not just a show of how well you can use profanity.

When you talk dirty, let your words reflect one or more of the following:

1. Appreciation for your partner:

Complement your partner's body parts, their looks, their sexiness, and how good you think they are at whatever it is they are doing to you or even to themselves. For example, "Your sexy goddess," "I totally adore your big cock," "You're so good with your tongue," or, "I can stare at your tits all day!"

Of course, you can include curse words when showing your appreciation. For example, "You're so fucking good," "Your nice little slut," or, "I love what you do to me with that damn dick of yours."

2. Describe how you feel:

Do not keep feelings locked up inside your head; go ahead and share them with your partner. For example, "I feel like coming when you stroke me that way," "Keep doing that baby, it feels so good," "Ummm... that's the spot," or, "I love your warm breath on my clit."

Describing how you feel has the following impacts:

- It tells your partner that you are enjoying what they are doing.

- It saves them the headache of guessing what you want and do not want.

- They can easily tune into you sexually by doing those things you enjoy.

- You get to connect and intensify your sexual feelings by simply describing them to your partner.

- You allow your partner to help you explore hidden parts of your sexuality that you may not have known to exist.

3. Describe what you want to do to your partner:

One of the powerful effects of talking dirty is building anticipation. When you describe what you are about to do or what you wish you could do to your partner, it helps their minds to create an imaginary and, perhaps, a more intense version of what you have described. Ordinarily, they may enjoy your touch for example, but adding a verbal description of how you want to touch them builds anticipation, directs their mind to your touch, and heightens the sensation of your touch because they have already imagined and felt it even before you touched them.

4. Ask your partner what they want:

Whether you are playing a submissive role, it is essential to have your partner's satisfaction in mind during sex and foreplay. So, your dirty talk should also include phrases that help your partner to say what they want. For example, "How would you like it, slow and gentle, or fast and rough?" "I'm here to please you, baby. Tell daddy what you want, and I'll do it," "Your wish is my fucking command," or, "Tell me your naughtiest fantasies and watch me bring them to reality."

Asking your partner what they want is not just to please them. You can also derive immense pleasure from pleasing your partner. Watching your partner have an earth-shaking orgasm because of something you did to them can also build your sexual confidence. Besides, your partner will hold you in sexual admiration. You know that they will be thinking about you sexually for a long time. Also, asking them what they want is the most direct way to remove the guesswork and do exactly what please them.

5. Tell your partner what you want:

Talking dirty is not just about pleasing your partner. It is also about getting as much sexual pleasure and stimulation as you can for yourself. A lot of women let themselves buy into the erroneous notion that dirty talk is all about pleasing their man alone. We all have desires whether we are men or women. Indeed, men are more sexually active for reasons. However, that does not diminish a woman's need for sexual pleasure.

Telling your partner what you want is about effective and loving communication. The goal is to help your partner give you sexual pleasure and satisfaction as you want it.

Note: There is no order for which you must use these suggestions. You do not have to always start from appreciating your partner, describing how you feel, and so on. The most important thing to keep in mind is that you are present with your feelings and bodily sensations, and you are letting yourself verbalize them freely. If something pops into your mind during sex (whether it is a question, a request, something you like or do not like), do not suppress it; say it.

Setting Personal Boundaries

Whatever you decide to settle for, always remember that dirty talks are supposed to increase fun, sexual excitement, intense pleasure, and comfortability. Anything that negates these will leave you with a less satisfying experience.

Think of setting personal boundaries as foreplay. Bring up the words you say to yourselves during sex and gauge your acceptance level in a relaxed way. Laugh about it, make silly faces if you must, and even tease each other about it. But make sure you let your partner know what you like and do not like and let them tell you what their boundaries are.

The following suggestions are meant to guide you in setting personal boundaries. Approach them with a mindset of ease and fun. If you think of them as iron-clad rules, you take away the fun and spontaneity from dirty talk. Approaching them as strict rules will limit you from exploring things that are seemingly off-limits for you now, but which may increase your sexual pleasure if you give them a try.

Go over what is comfortable

Everyone has a different tolerance level. What one person considers sexy; another considers offensive. For example, some people get turned on by aggressive sexuality and derogatory words such as, "whore," "slut," and "bitch." For other people, it is a complete no-no and a turn-off. It is up to you and your partner to go over what is comfortable for both of you and set acceptable "filthiness levels."

Profanity is not compulsory

You do not have to use profanity or vulgar words if you are not comfortable using them. For example, if you find the words "fuck," "cum," and "pussy juice" offensive, insulting, or disrespectful, it is okay to leave them out. However, saying things such as, "Make love to me," can only get you so far. You will have to push yourself to break free from being too conservative if you truly want wild and mind-blowing sex. Of course, you do not have to say the words that irritate you just to please your partner, but you could spice things up a little. For example, instead of saying, "Make love to me," you could say, "Baby, drive me crazy with your sweet lovemaking."

Do not be afraid to check in

It is a mark of respect for your partner to check in with their level of comfortability before using certain vulgar words for them.

When you are outside the bedroom and being sexual, you can ask them what they think about a phrase. Checking in with your partner shows that you want to say only the things that enhance your connection. For example, "How would you like it if I call you a dirty slut when I climax, tonight?" They may completely hate the idea and tell you so. They may love it and tell you so. Or they may want to make some adjustments like, "I prefer you call me 'your slut' instead of a 'dirty slut'."

It is not safe to assume that your partner will like everything you say simply because they love you and have been in a relationship with you for a while. If you make it a habit to check in with someone you just started dating recently, you increase your chances of having a healthy long-term relationship with them.

The type of relationship matters
Sexual relationships differ, and so should your choice of words. When you have sex with someone you just met or someone you are having a one-night stand with, it may not be a good idea to talk to them as if you know them.

It is safer to reserve sweet and loving words for long-term loving relationships such as a boyfriend and girlfriend relationship and a husband and wife relationship. Including sweet and loving words in your erotic talk increases the bond you share with your partner. If they are not someone you want to have a long-term relationship with, it is better to avoid using words such as "baby," "sweetie," honey," "darling," "cute," and so on.

Timing and frequency

While it is great to send raunchy texts and place calls to each other, it is equally important to respect each other's time. Let your partner know when it is okay to engage in phone sex and when you are busy doing other things. There should be mutual respect for your time online and offline.

As they say, too much of everything is bad. If every call and text is filled with gross, vulgar, and explicit words or images, you may soon lose interest.

Derogatory terms should be used only in private

The fact that you are comfortable with being called a "bitch," "slut," "whore," or a "playboy" in the bedroom doesn't mean that your partner should call you that outside the bedroom or in your normal conversations. Any reference to derogatory terms should be used strictly in private during sex, foreplay, or when they are trying to put you in the mood for sex using text and phone calls.

If your partner likes to be called a "dirty slut" during sex, it does not mean that is what they are in real-life and should not be treated as such. Even if you are not in a loving, long-term relationship with someone, treat them with respect regardless of what offensive words they enjoy during sex.

Keep information strictly private

The things you share in private are not subjects for conversation with anyone outside your relationship. Do not go telling your friends, "My boyfriend likes me to sit on his face and call him a wimp," or, "My girlfriend sent me her nudes last night." It is totally disrespectful and portrays you as someone who cannot be trusted with confidential information.

Also, do not threaten to share personal videos, pictures, text messages, or recorded phone calls with others. What you do with your partner is very private and should remain that way. If you both agree to a relationship that involves third parties or more, respect everyone in the relationship and keep private things private.